this OR that?
weather

tornado

OR

dust devil?

Josh Plattner

Consulting Editor, Diane Craig, M.A./Reading Specialist

Super Sandcastle

An Imprint of Abdo Publishing
abdopublishing.com

abdopublishing.com

Published by Abdo Publishing, a division of ABDO, PO Box 398166, Minneapolis, Minnesota 55439. Copyright © 2016 by Abdo Consulting Group, Inc. International copyrights reserved in all countries. No part of this book may be reproduced in any form without written permission from the publisher. Super SandCastle™ is a trademark and logo of Abdo Publishing.

Printed in the United States of America, North Mankato, Minnesota
102015
012016

Editor: Liz Salzmann
Content Developer: Nancy Tuminelly
Cover and Interior Design and Production: Mighty Media, Inc.
Photo Credits: Kelly Doudna, NASA, Shutterstock

Library of Congress Cataloging-in-Publication Data
Plattner, Josh, author.
  Tornado or dust devil? / Josh Plattner ; consulting editor, Diane Craig.
    pages cm -- (This or that? Weather)
  ISBN 978-1-62403-957-7
  1. Tornadoes--Juvenile literature. 2. Dust devils--Juvenile literature. I. Craig, Diane, editor. II. Title.
  QC955.2.P53 2016
  551.55'3--dc23
                    2015021244

Super SandCastle™ books are created by a team of professional educators, reading specialists, and content developers around five essential components—phonemic awareness, phonics, vocabulary, text comprehension, and fluency—to assist young readers as they develop reading skills and strategies and increase their general knowledge. All books are written, reviewed, and leveled for guided reading and early reading intervention programs for use in shared, guided, and independent reading and writing activities to support a balanced approach to literacy instruction.

contents

tornado or dust devil?

Is it a tornado? Or is it a dust devil? Do you know the difference?

A tornado is a **column** of air. The air spins. A tornado is **violent**.

A dust devil is also a **column** of air. It spins too. But a dust devil is not **violent**.

sky or ground?

A tornado forms in the sky. It hangs down from a cloud. It touches the ground.

A dust devil rises up from the earth. It forms on the ground. It stays on the ground.

what kind of weather?

Tornadoes are most common in spring and early summer. They form from big thunderstorms.

A tornado can look like a thin rope. It can look like a thick cone. Some tornadoes have more than one **column**.

Dust devils form in hot, dry air.
They form when there's no wind.
They form on flat, dry ground.

spin cycle

A tornado forms during a thunderstorm. The storm has different wind speeds inside it. The different speeds make the air spin. It spins faster and faster.

A **column** of spinning air drops from the cloud. This is the tornado. The tornado touches the ground. It destroys things in its way.

A dust devil happens when hot air rises. The hot air meets cooler air. The air begins to spin. The spinning air picks up dust and dirt from the ground.

turning time

Tornadoes can last for a few minutes. Some last longer. They spin at 75 miles per hour (120 kmh) or more.

Dust devils only last for about a minute. They are weak. They are small. They spin at 45 miles per hour (72 kmh) or less.

loco locations

Tornadoes can happen almost anywhere on Earth. But most tornadoes happen in North America. The middle United States is called "Tornado Alley."

Dust devils can form anywhere it is hot and dry. And they don't only form on Earth. There are dust devils on Mars!

what's it called?

Many tornadoes can form at once. This is called an outbreak. Outbreaks can have tens or even hundreds of tornadoes.

Dust devils are known by other names too. "Dancing devil" is from the United States. "Willy-willy" is from Australia.

at a glance

tornado —————— dust devil

tornado	dust devil
forms in the sky —————	forms on the ground
happens during a thunderstorm ———	happens on clear, hot days
caused by different ————— wind speeds	caused by different air temperatures
spins at 75 mph (120 kmh) or more —	spins at 45 mph (72 kmh) or less
most happen in North America ———	happens where it is hot and dry

soapy spinner

swirl up some suds in a false funnel.

What You'll Need
- empty plastic water bottle and cap
- water
- dish soap
- glitter

1. Put water in the bottle. Fill it two-thirds full.

2. Add two drops of dish **soap**.

3. Add a **pinch** of glitter. Glitter makes it easier to see the spinning.

4. Screw the cap on the bottle tightly.

5. **Swirl** the water in the bottle. Get it moving!

6. Look at the bottle. Can you see the "tornado"?

think about it

Why does the soap funnel form? How is the soap funnel like a real tornado?

glossary

column – a narrow pillar.

pinch – the amount you can hold between your thumb and one finger.

soap – a bar, liquid, or powder used to clean things.

swirl – to whirl or to move smoothly in circles.

violent – likely to attack or hurt others.